I0555285

THE
WONDERS
of
HEAVEN

The Key to this Treasure

Burl L. Shepard

WORDS MATTER
P U B L I S H I N G
OUR WORDS CHANGE THE WORLD

Words Matter Publishing
P.O. Box 1190
Decatur, IL 62525
www.wordsmatterpublishing.com

ISBN 13: 978-1-968542-08-5

Library of Congress Catalog Card Number: 2025948055

Table of Contents

CHAPTER 1

Treasure is defined as wealth or riches stored or accumulated. A treasure house is defined as a place or source where many things of value or worth may be found. The Holy Bible is the treasure of truth. The key to this treasure is Jesus Christ.

"He will be the sure foundation for your times, a rich store of salvation and wisdom and knowledge; the fear of the Lord is the key to this treasure." — *Isaiah 33:6 (NIV)*

"My purpose is that they may be encouraged in heart and united in love, so that they may have the full riches of complete understanding, in order that they may know the mystery of God, namely Christ, in whom are hidden all the treasures of wisdom and knowledge." — *Colossians 2:2-3 (NIV)*

Billy Graham, in one of his bestselling books, *Death and the Life After*, makes reference to a person who wrote about the wonders of heaven. The following few pages are from this book:

"In heaven, there will be no more sorrowful separations. For many people, life on earth has lost its meaning because dear ones or close friends who were a vital part of life on earth are no longer here. In heaven, we will be together in Christ. We will see the mother or father, the children, brothers, or sisters who have preceded us. We will have a family reunion like no other!"

Even when we allow our imaginations to run wild on the joys of heaven, we find that our minds are incapable of conceiving what it will really be like. We are imprisoned by our earthly limitations. Years ago, Rebecca Ruter Springer wrote a little book called *My Dream of Heaven.* One of my friends told me she was given a copy of the book after the death of a loved one, and it soothed her by describing the glories of heaven in such a beautiful way that she could appreciate and even anticipate what wonders her loved one was enjoying.

The book, in its quaint early 19th-century style, was fanciful, but it captured biblical truths with emotional impressions. We wonder, for instance, about some of the things we loved on earth. Will we be separated from them in heaven? What about our favorite pets? Is there a place for them? I don't know the exact answers to those questions, but I trust the love of my Lord. Everything needed for our happiness will be there.

In describing her journey *Intra Muros* (within the gates), Mrs. Springer wrote:

> "Do you know, I think one of the sweetest proofs we have of our Father's loving care for us is that we so often find in this life the things which gave us great happiness below. The more unexpected this is, the greater joy it brings. I remember once seeing a beautiful little girl in heaven, the

very first to come of a large and affectionate family. Afterward, I learned that the sorrowful cry of her mother was, *Oh, if only we had someone there to meet her, to care for her!*

'She came lovingly nestled in the Master's own arms, and a little later, as He sat still caressing and talking to her, a remarkably fine Angora kitten—of which the child had been very fond and which had sickened and died some weeks before to her great sorrow—came running across the grass and sprang directly into her arms, where it lay contentedly.

'Such a glad cry as she recognized her little favorite! Such hugging and kissing as that kitten received made joy even in heaven!'

Far-fetched? Why should it be? If to die is gain as Paul said, then why shouldn't we enjoy even more in heaven the things that we loved on earth?

It is often asked: Will we be married in heaven? The Sadducees of Jesus' time questioned Him about a woman who had seven husbands. They asked:

> "At the resurrection, whose wife will she be, since the seven were married to her?"

Jesus replied:

> "Are you not in error because you do not know the Scriptures or the power of God? When the dead rise, they will

neither marry nor be given in marriage; they will be like the angels in heaven." — *Mark 12:23-25 (NIV)*

Someone may object, *but I love my husband or wife so much. If we know our loved ones in heaven, why aren't we married?* There are also instances in which a person has had more than one marriage, as did the woman to whom the Sadducees referred.

The more I meditate on the promises of heaven, the more I have faith that these questions will no longer be relevant because they will be answered in a glorious manner. I trust Jesus with all my tomorrows, knowing that He will solve the mystery of life beyond the grave.

— *Death and the Life After*, Paperback Edition, pp. 175-176

***

A Bible verse that is often misquoted—perhaps more than any other—is "Money is the root of all evil." Actually, money is something we need very much, and its usefulness is often spoken about in the Bible. When used correctly, money brings many blessings. Money itself is not the root of all evil. The correct quote is:

"People who want to get rich fall into temptation and a trap and into many foolish and harmful desires that plunge men into ruin and destruction. For the love of money is the root of all kinds of evil." — *1 Timothy 6:9-10 (NIV)*

"No one can serve two masters. Either he will hate the one and love the other, or he will be devoted to the one and despise the other. You cannot serve both God and money."
— *Matthew 6:24 (NIV)*

The love of money can draw one into a trap from which it is difficult to escape. It can lead to alcohol and drug abuse, addiction to gambling, pornography, and prostitutes in order to satisfy lustful desires. This leads to child abuse, broken families, and much more. The love of money is an avenue for Satan to draw people into depravity that leads to destruction and hell.

On the other hand, when used as God intended, money brings many blessings. The satisfaction we feel from providing for our families is an excellent example. It is natural to utilize our money for the welfare of our families, according to how much God has blessed us. There are numerous ways to use our money for the goodness of God. The needy can be helped in a variety of ways, and God knows there are many who desperately need help.

Money may also be donated to pro-life centers to pay for sonograms for expectant mothers. It is said that a high percentage of women contemplating abortion decide to keep their precious babies when they see their baby and hear its heartbeat for the first time. Donations can also help purchase diapers, baby formula, cribs, blankets, and other necessities.

God has blessed some with more financial resources than others. For such people, it would be wise to increase their giving. As an example, I've heard it said that a donation of around $15,000 will purchase an ultrasound machine. It would not be unreasonable for those who can afford it to donate funds for more than one machine. This generous act would display wisdom on their part, for the value of human life cannot be measured. In heaven, compound interest will begin to accumulate on their generosity long before they arrive and will continue throughout eternity.

How should one decide how much to give and where to give? Follow your heart as the Holy Spirit speaks to you.

"Jesus sat down opposite the place where the offerings were put and watched the crowd putting their money into the temple treasury. Many rich people threw in large amounts. But a poor widow came and put in two very small copper coins, worth only a fraction of a penny. Calling His disciples to Him, Jesus said, 'I tell you the truth, this poor widow has put more into the treasury than all the others. They all gave out of their wealth; but she, out of her poverty, put in everything—all she had to live on.'" — *Mark 12:41-44 (NIV)*

No person is excluded in their desire to advance the kingdom of God. All who give with a glad heart will be greatly rewarded.

It is difficult to adjust to the loss of a spouse. At the time of this writing, my wife, Marilyn, has been in the presence of the Lord for close to five years. To me, it feels more like fifty. However, I believe she is very happy as well as very safe, and I praise God for that. I also believe she is experiencing time in heaven much differently than I do on earth. When we are reunited in heaven, it will seem to her that only a short time has passed.

There are special moments I miss in regard to my wife, and I'm certain this is true for many whose spouses are now waiting in heaven. While some might think these moments were meaningless or even foolish, they held meaning only for the two of us.

On my part, these moments could be described as playful arrogance. For example, on rare occasions, I would come up with a good idea for handling a particular problem or situation, and my wife would reluctantly have to agree. Seeing her agreement, I would sit with my chest puffed out, a smug smile on my face, and declare, "I'm pretty smart." The look I received from her in those moments was priceless—somewhere between apathy and pity, leaning more toward pity.

My wife was also very good at coming up with problem-solving solutions. Sometimes, it was as simple as deciding which route to take on a three-day getaway. She would describe the different sights we'd see and things we could do along a particular route. When her narrative was finished, I would sit in deep thought for a moment, pretending to ponder her suggestion. Then, after a pause, I'd say, "I know!" and repeat her exact words back to her, ending with. "Wow, that was a brilliant idea I came up with! I don't know why I didn't think of it sooner."

Her response was another priceless look, followed by an eye roll and a slow shake of her head. She would say nothing, but

I could see her resolve not to fall into my trap again. Yet, with time, she invariably would, giving me the opportunity to enjoy another special moment.

These moments were uniquely ours, and while I miss them, I am grateful for every one of them.

CHAPTER 2

What is the Judgment Seat of God, and what is its purpose? The Judgment Seat of God has nothing to do with a believer losing their salvation. Once saved by the blood of Jesus through the power of the Gospel, one's salvation cannot be lost. The judgment of God will be conducted by Jesus, and rewards will be given in accordance with each believer's service to God while on earth. Some will receive much, and some will receive little. Others may be asked why they did not do more with the opportunities they were given to serve God.

There will be those who might have been in compromising situations at the moment of the rapture who will feel great embarrassment and shame in the presence of the Master.

"Therefore keep watch, because you do not know on what day your Lord will come." — *Matthew 24:42 (NIV)*

This will be an incredible event, unlike anything ever experienced on earth. It will include the Redeemer, Jesus Christ, and the redeemed—those bought and paid for by His blood. There will be a great multitude of the redeemed, but sadly, an even more multitudinous number of unbelievers will be missing. These will find themselves in Hades, the realm of the dead, as they await the Great White Throne Judgment, which will occur after the second coming of Christ.

"Enter through the narrow gate. For wide is the gate and broad is the road that leads to destruction, and many enter through it. But small is the gate and narrow the road that leads to life, and only a few find it." — *Matthew 7:13-14 (NIV)*

In my mind's eye, I imagine an example inspired by Billy Graham. Far-fetched? Why should it be? This is what I see occurring at the judgment seat of God:

> The redeemed man sat in awe and amazement at what was transpiring before his eyes. Row upon row of innumerable seats stretched before him, each row slightly higher than the one before. The seats were perfectly positioned for viewing the grand stage that was far above his particular vantage point. He realized the distance of the stage mattered not, for he instantly knew that he would see the stage no better if he were in the first row and no worse if he were in the last. Everyone was equal in the sight of God and would be treated as such.

The man marveled as he watched the seats fill with redeemed men and women. There were no aisles in the great arena to provide access to the seats because no aisles were needed. Neither had notices been posted, nor speakers heard blaring to announce it was time for the event to begin. The other redeemed men and women, like him, simply knew in their minds that it was time. Although they didn't fully understand how, they found themselves traveling from their previous locations in heaven to the seats that had been reserved for them since before their birth.

"Before I formed you in the womb, I knew you; before you were born, I set you apart." — *Jeremiah 1:5 (NIV)*

The redeemed man found heaven to be life at its best—the way it was meant to be. He quickly conformed to his heavenly existence. His moments with Jesus were awe-inspiring, and his glimpses of the beauty and glory of God, along with the love that radiated from Him, were a blissful mixture of inexpressible emotions. His interactions with other heavenly beings were gratifying, fulfilling his desire for godly and harmonious relationships.

The redeemed man knew he could fully trust his Lord and Savior, for Jesus had done exactly as He said in His Holy Word:

> "Do not let your hearts be troubled. Trust in God; trust also in Me. In My Father's house are many rooms; if it were not so, I would have told you. I am going there to prepare a place for you. And if I go and prepare a place for you, I will come back and take you to be with Me that you also may be where I am." — *John 14:1-3 (NIV)*

Jesus had indeed gone to prepare a place for him and then returned to take him to heaven at the rapture. Therefore, the redeemed man had a place to live in heaven—an established residence that was his alone, used for godly interaction with other redeemed believers. During these moments, much laughter could be heard. Prayer, meditation, and the enjoyment of godly music were common.

He was in no way confined to his residence, he could come and go as he pleased. Yet, it was a permanent home that declared, *I belong here. I am home.*

As the redeemed man contemplated the joy, happiness, and fulfillment he had experienced since the rapture—including fellowship with born-again family members—he realized something was missing. There was a void that lay between him and a very important memory. No matter how hard he tried to recall it, he kept drawing blanks. He found this quite perplexing and determined to soon discuss the matter with the Lord Jesus.

But for now, the Judgment Seat of God was about to begin, and all his thoughts turned to the matter at hand. As the man watched the seats before him fill with believers, the seat on his right suddenly became occupied. The redeemed woman who appeared beside him lightly brushed against his arm. This slight contact caused a pleasant tingling sensation to surge through the redeemed man's glorified body.

With a smile on his face, he turned to acknowledge her arrival. When their eyes met, time seemed to stand still. In that instant, the redeemed man realized what had been missing—he was gazing into the eyes of his earthly spouse, who had preceded him to the heavenly realm. She, too, was taken aback by this unexpected reunion, for the Lord had also withheld the memory of her former spouse from her mind.

Suddenly, the magnificent Jesus appeared on the great rostrum high above them. His eyes, full of merriment and love, seemed to bore into their own. A ripple of joy spread throughout the grand stadium. The two of them instantly knew that many other former spouses were also experiencing this wonderful gift.

While not everyone is meant for an eternal soulmate relationship, there are many who are. After the proceedings of the Judgment Seat of God are finished, those who have been reunited with their earthly spouses will return together to the husband's residence in heaven. This will now be their eternal home as they experience the treasures of Jesus and His kingdom throughout the universe.

"The Son is the radiance of God's glory and the exact representation of His being, sustaining all things by His powerful word." — *Hebrews 1:3 (NIV)*

The following lyrics from a beautiful song capture the essence of the rapture:

I can hear a distant cry, shouting out the time is nigh,
As the Father tells His Son, "Work on earth this day is done.
Son, go bring My children home, for I want them gathered around My throne.
It's time to reap the harvest You have sown.
Son, go bring My children home."

What a joy to see His face; in His arms we will embrace,
Nevermore will we have to roam, for we've finally made it home.
Son, go bring My children home.
The Coblentz Family

One of two events will occur that will pave the way for my wife and me to be reunited: either the rapture will happen, or the appointed time God has set for the death of my physical body will arrive.

"There is a time for everything, and a season for every activity under heaven: a time to be born and a time to die."
— *Ecclesiastes 3:1-2 (NIV)*

I have accepted the free gift of salvation God has provided by asking for forgiveness of my sins and accepting His Son, Jesus, as Lord of my life—just as my wife did before her passing. Therefore, heaven is assured.

"For it is by grace you have been saved, through faith—and this not from yourselves, it is the gift of God—not by works, so that no one can boast." — *Ephesians 2:8-9 (NIV)*

Over the ages, whenever the physical death of believers occurred, their souls immediately entered the presence of the Lord in heaven. There, they live productive and meaningful lives, full of wonderment and love. When the rapture occurs, all the spirits residing in heaven will accompany Jesus to the airspace surrounding the Earth. At that moment, the remains of their physical bodies will be reunited and joined with their spirits, and they will receive glorified bodies similar to the glorified body of Christ. There are some who believe that the dead bodies are being held in a mass grave, supernaturally prepared by Jesus as they await the resurrection. Ultimately, the condition of the bodies—or even if they were completely destroyed—does not matter.

Following this, all believers who are alive on the Earth will be taken up and will also receive glorified bodies. All will then return to heaven with Jesus. This incredible event will occur in the blink of an eye, causing great confusion on Earth for those who are left behind.

"Listen, I tell you a mystery: We will not all sleep, but we will all be changed—in a flash, in the twinkling of an eye, at the last trumpet. For the trumpet will sound, the dead will be raised imperishable, and we will be changed." — *1 Corinthians 15:51-52 (NIV)*

"According to the Lord's own word, we tell you that we who are still alive, who are left till the coming of the Lord, will certainly not precede those who have fallen asleep. For the Lord Himself will come down from heaven, with a loud command, with the voice of the archangel and with the trumpet call of God, and the dead in Christ will rise first. After that, we who are still alive and are left will be caught up together with them in the clouds to meet the Lord in the air. And so we will be with the Lord forever." — *1 Thessalonians 4:15-17 (NIV)*

During the rapture, an unbelieving mother holding her baby will suddenly find her arms empty. An unbelieving father sitting at the breakfast table, watching his redeemed wife feeding their child, will suddenly find himself alone. A non-Christian who needs to fly during these end times might pray an oxymoronic prayer—that the pilot and copilot are unbelievers—for if the rapture occurs mid-flight, the plane would surely crash, as no plane can fly and land itself safely.

But what about those who died before the virgin birth of Jesus and His death and resurrection? Are they without hope?

"If, in fact, Abraham was justified by works, he had something to boast about—but not before God. What does the Scripture say? 'Abraham believed God, and it was credited to him as righteousness.'" — *Romans 4:2-3 (NIV)*

"Now faith is being sure of what we hope for and certain of what we do not see. This is what the ancients were commended for." — *Hebrews 11:1-2 (NIV)*

There are those who believe that the saints of God will be judged at a different time. Before the Judgment Seat of God, the rapture, the Tribulation, and Great Tribulation—also known as the seven-year period or "Jacob's trouble"—will occur. The first half of this period appears to bring peace, but is actually filled with deceit from the enemies of God. During the second half of this seven-year period, God will pour out His wrath upon the earth. Only the Second Coming of Jesus will prevent the earth from complete destruction.

"For then there will be great distress, unequaled from the beginning of the world until now—and never to be equaled again. If those days had not been cut short, no one would survive, but for the sake of the elect those days will be shortened." — *Matthew 24:21-22 (NIV)*

The rapture is clear evidence that the Church—believers in Christ worldwide throughout all ages—will not suffer through the Tribulation and Great Tribulation.

"For God did not appoint us to suffer wrath but to receive salvation through our Lord Jesus Christ. He died for us so that, whether we are awake or asleep, we may live together with Him." — *1 Thessalonians 5:9-10 (NIV)*

In the Bible, the word "asleep" refers to the physical body at the time of death. The spirit of believers immediately enters heaven at death. Indeed, heaven is merely a heartbeat away.

CHAPTER 3

During the Second Coming, those who were raptured will return to the Earth with Jesus. They will not participate in battle, but will instead observe as Satan is bound by a great chain and thrown into the abyss for one thousand years. This period is referred to as the Millennial Kingdom, during which Jesus will rule on Earth.

"And I saw an angel coming down out of heaven, having the key to the Abyss and holding in his hand a great chain. He seized the dragon, that ancient serpent, who is the devil, or Satan, and bound him for a thousand years. He threw him into the Abyss, and locked and sealed it over him, to keep him from deceiving the nations anymore until the thousand years were ended. After that, he must be set free for a short time." — *Revelation 20:1–3 (NIV)*

I have heard it said that Jesus will need the help of the raptured to restore the Earth to a livable condition. This is not a true statement. Why do I say this? It is because Jesus does not need anything. It was He who created the world and everything in it. It was also He who caused the destruction of the Great Tribulation to occur. Therefore, He is more than capable of restoring the Earth to a far better condition.

"The Son is the radiance of God's glory and the exact representation of His being, sustaining all things by His powerful word." — *Hebrews 1:3 (NIV)*

However, we will indeed be involved in the restoration of the Earth. Why would Jesus allow us to do so? Because it is about us in the first place. We are the very reason for His terrible suffering and death on the cross. Jesus was the ransom paid by God to deliver us from punishment for our sins.

We will participate during the Millennium on planet Earth. How might Jesus choose to involve us in restoring the Earth? Will He select people for tasks matching their earthly work history? Will those with knowledge of farming be used to revive agriculture? Will electricians restore power grids and bring them back online? Or might Jesus grant us supernatural powers to quickly bring order and restoration? However, He chooses to accomplish this, it will be done quickly and efficiently.

The Millennial period on Earth will be unique. There will be both the redeemed—those raptured, possessing glorified bodies that do not have the ability to procreate—as well as those who survive the Tribulation with normal human bodies. Countless numbers of people will have been killed during the Tribulation, yet those who survive will repopulate the Earth. Many of these survivors will accept Jesus as Savior and Lord. Although they are saved, they cannot transfer their salvation to their children, for each person must individually ask for salvation. Salvation cannot be obtained collectively.

CHAPTER 4

Johnny Cash, an entertainer beloved by many, performed a variety of secular songs. *"One Piece at a Time"* was a favorite during the mid-1970s. It tells the humorous story of a man who left Kentucky in 1949 and traveled to Detroit, where he landed a job on an assembly line producing Cadillacs. He greatly admired these beautiful cars and devised a plan to acquire one for himself, free of charge.

His scheme was to sneak parts out every workday, one piece at a time, so that by the time he retired, he would have his dream car. An oversized lunchbox was used for smaller items, such as gears, shocks, fuel pumps, lights, and so forth. Larger items like the engine and transmission were smuggled out with the help of his friends and transported in a buddy's mobile home.

Lyrics from the song humorously state:

> *"I've never considered myself a thief, but GM wouldn't miss just one little piece, especially if I strung it out over several years."*

He explained that the plan worked well until he and his friends attempted to assemble the car. They quickly discovered that the transmission was from a '53 model, while the motor came from a '73, causing nothing to fit properly. However, with an adapter kit and by drilling new holes, the engine was soon running, "just like a song."

Further problems arose. For instance, the vehicle had two headlights on the left and one on the right, though he was quick to proudly add, "All three burned." Additionally, the back end appeared strange because it had only one tail fin. When he and his wife drove uptown to register the car, they could hear everyone laughing—though no laughter came from the courthouse clerk who had to issue the title, which weighed "sixty pounds."

The chorus proudly states:

> *"I got it one piece at a time, and it didn't cost me a dime.*
> *You'll know it's me when I come through your town.*
> *I'm gonna ride around in style, I'm gonna drive everybody wild,*
> *'Cause I'll have the only one there is around."*

"One Piece at a Time" is indeed a delightfully funny song guaranteed to make one laugh, yet it clearly illustrates how easily we rationalize behaviors that do not align with God's moral law. No matter how likable the factory worker in the song was, he still broke several of God's commandments. He had made an idol of the car, stolen parts to assemble it, and coveted what was not his own.

This humorous tale highlights humanity's predicament when facing a righteous God who demands perfection. However, once redeemed by the blood of Jesus, a true believer genuinely desires to follow God's commandments, even in the smallest details of life.

For example, imagine an office worker who, after returning home from work, realizes he has inadvertently placed four paper clips into his shirt pocket during the day. As a committed Christian, instead of casually tossing them onto his dresser, he carefully sets them aside to return the next morning. This Christian maintains the same mindset regarding petty cash at work; though a few dollars might never be missed, misusing any amount would be theft. And consider an honor system for coffee—one might think, "Who would know if I poured a cup without paying?" The answer is clear: God would know.

"One Piece at a Time," artist Johnny Cash (1976). Songwriter: Wayne Kemp.

Another favorite song by Johnny Cash is *"A Boy Named Sue."* This song is about a rowdy, tough, hoodlum father who deserted his wife and three-year-old son. As the son, now a grown man, explains in the song:

"Now I don't blame him 'cause he ran and hid,
But the meanest thing that my daddy ever did,
Was before he left, he went and named me Sue."

Later in the song, the grown son finally encounters his father. This chance meeting occurs in a bar, leading to a fierce confrontation. During their fight, the father reveals his reasoning:

"Son, this world is rough, and if a man's gonna make it, he's gotta be tough.

I knew I wouldn't be there to help you along,

So I gave you that name and I said goodbye.

I knew you'd have to get tough or die;

It's that name that helped to make you strong."

Near the end, the son concludes humorously:

"If I ever have a boy, I'll name him Frank or George or Bill or Tom—anything but Sue!"

Although this song was very popular during its time, it contains words and expressions many would now find offensive. My purpose in referencing this song is to highlight the dramatic cultural changes in America during the approximately fifty years since it was written. In the mid-1970s, traditional masculine qualities of manhood were admired and respected. To call a man "Sue" or any other feminine name would have been a deep insult.

Today, however, men are frequently attacked or criticized for their God-given masculinity. As a result, many men prefer to remain hidden in the shadows, neglecting their responsibilities to their wives and children. Even more troubling are those who openly deny their manhood, choosing instead to identify by a feminine name like "Sue." Indeed, we are living in sorrowful and regrettable times.

and He will make your paths straight." — *Proverbs 3:5–6 (NIV)*

"For a man's ways are in full view of the Lord, and He examines all his paths." — *Proverbs 5:21 (NIV)*

"A gentle answer turns away wrath, but a harsh word stirs up anger." — *Proverbs 15:1 (NIV)*

"A man's steps are directed by the Lord. How then can anyone understand his own way?" — *Proverbs 20:24 (NIV)*

From Ecclesiastes:

"I devoted myself to study and to explore by wisdom all that is done under heaven. What a heavy burden God has laid on men! I have seen all the things that are done under the sun; all of them are meaningless, a chasing after the wind." — *Ecclesiastes 1:13–14 (NIV)*

"As you do not know the path of the wind or how the body is formed in a mother's womb, so you cannot understand the work of God, the Maker of all things." — *Ecclesiastes 11:5 (NIV)*

"Now all has been heard; here is the conclusion of the matter: Fear God and keep His commandments, for this is the whole duty of man. For God will bring every deed into judgment, including every hidden thing, whether it is good or evil." — *Ecclesiastes 12:13–14 (NIV)*

God speaks to humanity through the Bible, using the common language of our days. One need not understand ancient Hebrew or Greek to grasp the truths of His Holy Word.

Imagine, for a moment, a non-believer—a man who had never heard the Gospel—shipwrecked on a deserted island. One day, while exploring his surroundings, the shipwrecked man spots a strange object partially hidden by grass and vines. Realizing it is some sort of book, the man carefully removes it from its entanglement. As he brushes away the dirt, he notices the title on the front cover: "The Message."

Puzzled but curious, the man walks to a small grove of trees, sits in the shade, and begins reading. He quickly finds himself fascinated by the writings. Afternoon soon turns to dusk, and as darkness falls, the man rises and returns to the small hut he had constructed for shelter. That night, he falls asleep, tightly clutching the book to his chest.

As the days pass, the shipwrecked man continues reading, gradually becoming aware of a presence filled with peace and love. Though he knows he might spend the rest of his days alone on this deserted island, he now feels genuine hope—and from that hope comes the strength to carry on. He realizes he has discovered something infinitely precious: the One who inspired this book, written through mortal men chosen by God Himself.

What follows are selections of Scripture, randomly chosen and presented from *The Message*, an interpretation of the Bible in contemporary, everyday language.

Genesis 1:1–3 (MSG)

> "First this: God created the Heavens and Earth—all you see, all you don't see.
>
> Earth was a soup of nothingness, a bottomless emptiness, an inky blackness.
>
> God's Spirit brooded like a bird above the watery abyss.
>
> God spoke: 'Light!' And light appeared."

Genesis 12:1–3 (MSG)

"God told Abram:

> 'Leave your country, your family, and your father's home for a land that I will show you.
>
> I'll make you a great nation and bless you.
>
> I'll make you famous; you'll be a blessing.
>
> I'll bless those who bless you; those who curse you, I'll curse.
>
> All the families of the Earth will be blessed through you."

Exodus 20:1–17 (MSG)

"God spoke all these words:

> 'I am God, your God, who brought you out of the land of Egypt, out of a life of slavery.
>
> No other gods, only Me.

No carved gods of any size, shape, or form of anything whatever.

No using the name of God, your God, in curses or silly banter.

Observe the Sabbath day, to keep it holy.

Honor your father and mother.

No murder.

No adultery.

No stealing.

No lies about your neighbor.

No lusting after your neighbor's house—or wife or servant or maid."

"But now I have chosen both a city and a person: Jerusalem for honoring My name, and David to lead My people Israel." — *2 Chronicles 6:6 (MSG)*

"If I ever shut off the supply of rain from the skies or order the locusts to eat the crops, or send a plague on My people, and My people—My God-defined people—respond by humbling themselves, praying, seeking My presence, and turning their backs on their wicked lives, I'll be there ready for you. I'll listen from heaven, forgive their sins, and restore their land to health." — *2 Chronicles 7:14 (MSG)*

"Count yourself lucky, how happy you must be—

You get a fresh start,

Your slate's wiped clean.

Count yourself lucky—

God holds nothing against you.

And you're holding nothing back from Him."

— Psalm 32:1–2 (MSG)

"You who sit down in the High God's presence,

Spend the night in Shaddai's shadow,

Say this:

'God, You're my refuge.

I trust in You and I'm safe!"

— Psalm 91:1–2 (MSG)

"Investigate my life, O God,

Find out everything about me;

Cross-examine and test me,

Get a clear picture of what I'm about;

See for Yourself whether I've done anything wrong—

Then guide me on the road to eternal life."

— Psalm 139:23–24 (MSG)

"The Word that saves is right here,

As near as the tongue in your mouth,

As close as the heart in your chest.

It's the word of faith that welcomes God to go to work and set things right for us.

This is the core of our preaching.

Say the welcoming word to God—'Jesus is my Master'

Embracing, body and soul, God's work of doing in us what He did in raising Jesus from the dead.

> That's it. You're not 'doing' anything;
> You're simply calling out to God,
> Trusting Him to do it for you.
> That's salvation."

— Romans 10:9–10 (MSG)

"The experts of our day haven't a clue about what this eternal plan is.

If they had, they wouldn't have killed the Master of the God-designed life on a cross.

That's why we have this Scripture text:

> 'No one's ever seen or heard anything like this,
> Never so much as imagined anything quite like it—
> What God has arranged for those who love Him."

— 1 Corinthians 2:8–10 (MSG)

"Come. Sit down.

Let's argue this out.

This is God's Message:

'If your sins are blood-red,

They'll be snow-white.

If they're red like crimson,

They'll be like wool."

— Isaiah 1:18 (MSG)

"I am most emphatic here, friends:

This great Message I deliver to you is not mere human optimism.

I didn't receive it through the traditions,

And I wasn't taught it in some school.

I got it straight from God—

Received the Message directly from Jesus Christ."

— Galatians 1:11–12 (MSG)

He wants not only us, but everyone to be saved. He wants everyone to get to know the truth.

"We've learned that there is one God and only one, and one Priest-Mediator between God and us—Jesus, who offered Himself in exchange for everyone held captive by sin, to set them all free." *— 1 Timothy 2:5 (MSG)*

"For a Child has been born—for us!

The gift of a Son—for us!

He'll take over the running of the world.

His name will be: Amazing Counselor,

Strong God,

Eternal Father,

Prince of Wholeness.

His ruling authority will grow,

And there'll be no limits to the wholeness He brings.

He'll rule from the historic David throne over that promised kingdom.

He'll put that kingdom on a firm footing and keep it going.

With fair dealing and right living,

Beginning now and lasting always.

The zeal of God-of-the-Angel-Armies will do all this."

— Isaiah 9:6–7 (MSG)

"So turn to Me and be helped—saved!—everyone, whoever and wherever you are.

I am God, the only God there is, the One and only.

I promise in My own name: Every word out of My mouth does what it says.

I never take back what I say.

Everyone is going to end up kneeling before Me.

Everyone is going to end up saying of Me,

'Yes! Salvation and strength are in God!"

— Isaiah 45:22–23 (MSG)

"Before I shaped you in the womb, I knew all about you.

Before you saw the light of day, I had holy plans for you."

— Jeremiah 1:5 (MSG)

"The Word was first,

The Word present to God,

God present to the Word.

The Word was God,

In readiness for God from day one.

Everything was created through Him;

Nothing—not one thing—came into being without Him.

What came into existence was Life,

And the Life was Light to live by.

The Life-Light blazed out of the darkness;

The darkness couldn't put it out."

— John 1:1–5 (MSG)

"This is how much God loved the world: He gave His Son, His one and only Son.

And this is why: so that no one need be destroyed;

By believing in Him, anyone can have a whole and lasting life.

God didn't go to all the trouble of sending His Son merely to point an accusing finger,

Telling the world how bad it was.

He came to help,

To put the world right again.

Anyone who trusts in Him is acquitted;

Anyone who refuses to trust Him has long since been under the death sentence without knowing it.

And why? Because of that person's failure to believe in the one-of-a-kind Son of God when introduced to Him."

— *John 3:16 (MSG)*

"You don't have to wait for the end.

I am, right now, Resurrection and Life.

The one who believes in Me, even though he or she dies, will live.

And everyone who lives believing in Me does not ultimately die at all."

— *John 11:25–26 (MSG)*

"Don't let this throw you.

You trust God, don't you? Trust Me.

There is plenty of room for you in My Father's home.

If that weren't so, would I have told you that I'm on My way to get a room ready for you?

And if I'm on My way to get your room ready, I'll come back and get you

So you can live where I live.

And you already know the road I'm taking."

— John 14:1–4 (MSG)

"You don't know the first thing about tomorrow.

You're nothing but a wisp of fog,

Catching a brief bit of sun before disappearing."

— James 4:14 (MSG)

"I give fair warning to all who hear the words of the prophecy of this book:

If you add to the words of this prophecy, God will add to your life the disasters written in this book.

If you subtract from the words of this prophecy,

God will subtract your part from the Tree of Life and the Holy City that are written in this book.

He who testifies to all these things says it again:

> 'I'm on My way! I'll be there soon!'
> Yes! Come, Master Jesus!
> The grace of the Master Jesus be with all of you.
> Oh, yes!"

— Revelation 22:18–21 (MSG)

But what if something happened to *The Message*? What if someone came along and destroyed it?

Imagine a band of monkeys finding the book and fighting over its possession. During their noisy dispute, all of the pages were ripped from *The Message* and scattered by the wind. When the shipwrecked man later found it, all that remained was the badly torn book cover. Wondering what it might have contained, he tossed it aside and continued on his way.

Had the shipwrecked man lost his only opportunity to find God?

Our sovereign God has many ways of reaching one in need of His salvation. For example, the deserted island was free from artificial light, allowing the man a clear, unobstructed view of the night sky. As days and nights passed, he observed the heavens with amazement and awe. Slowly, he began to realize there was much more to existence than himself.

In this way, he came to the conclusion that he had found the One of whom there can be no higher. He realized he was in desperate need of this great Being. And so, through creation, dreams, and the quiet voice of the Spirit, the shipwrecked man came to know his Savior.

"The heavens declare the glory of God;
The skies proclaim the work of His hands.

Day after day they pour forth speech;
Night after night they display knowledge.

There is no speech or language where their voice is not heard.

Their voice goes out into all the earth,
Their words to the ends of the world."

— Psalm 19:1–4 (NIV)

CHAPTER 6

Mantras, Meditation, and the Message of Life

It is not wrong to use mantras when worshiping God. However, the repetition should have meaning and not consist of vain, empty, or useless verbiage. Genuine comfort and peace can be found by repeating a passage of Scripture that holds special meaning to you.

If the worries of this fallen world cause sleeplessness, one might try a repetitive session of prayer. A good starting place may be the words Jesus taught His disciples to pray:

"Our Father which art in Heaven,

Hallowed be Thy name.

Thy kingdom come,

Thy will be done on earth as it is in Heaven.

Give us this day our daily bread.

And forgive us our debts, as we forgive our debtors.

And lead us not into temptation,

But deliver us from evil:

For Thine is the kingdom, and the power, and the glory, forever. Amen."

— Matthew 6:9–13 (KJV)

"I will lie down and sleep in peace,

For you alone, O Lord, make me dwell in safety."

— Psalm 4:8 (NIV)

"The Lord is my shepherd, I shall not be in want.

He makes me lie down in green pastures,

He leads me beside quiet waters,

He restores my soul.

He guides me in paths of righteousness for His name's sake.

Even though I walk through the valley of the shadow of death,

I will fear no evil, for You are with me;

Your rod and Your staff, they comfort me.

You prepare a table before me in the presence of my enemies.

You anoint my head with oil; my cup overflows.

Surely goodness and love will follow me all the days of my life,

And I will dwell in the house of the Lord forever."

— Psalm 23 (NIV)

Postmillennialism holds the belief that humanity will experience a thousand-year period of peace on Earth, ushered in by the church itself. At the end of the thousand years, Satan will be released, and only then will Christ return to defeat Satan and establish His eternal reign. According to this view, the Second Coming of Christ occurs after the thousand-year period. However, this position is very easy to refute by simply looking at reality. The Earth has been anything but peaceful and harmonious throughout the church age and is currently headed toward total destruction at an accelerated pace. Humanity has been infected with sin since the fall in the Garden of Eden. Standing naked before God does not merely refer to being unclothed but rather standing shamefully before Him, completely exposed in our transgressions. It has been rightly said that although humanity is not worthy, humanity has tremendous worth to God.

Premillennialism also views the thousand years as a literal period of time, but believes Christ's Second Coming will usher in His thousand-year reign on Earth and that this event occurs before the final removal of Satan. This interpretation carries the most credibility and aligns closely with Biblical prophecy.

Amillennialism interprets the thousand-year period as symbolic, representing the time between Christ's ascension and His return. In this view, the Millennium is Christ reigning spiritually in the hearts of believers and within His church. Essentially, this position equates the Millennium with the current church age, which will conclude with Christ's Second Coming. However, this interpretation fails to fully account for specific Biblical prophecies, such as Isaiah 9:6–7.

We must understand that God's ways serve as our ultimate moral example. It is God's law that makes us aware of sin.

"Therefore no one will be declared righteous in His sight by observing the law; rather, through the law we become conscious of sin." — *Romans 3:20 (NIV)*

Without God's moral law, people are left to create their own definitions of good and evil—an unfortunate reality faced by multitudes today.

The Ten Commandments

1. You shall have no other gods before Me.
2. You shall not make for yourselves an idol in the form of anything.
3. You shall not misuse the name of the Lord your God.
4. Remember the Sabbath day by keeping it holy.
5. Honor your father and your mother.
6. You shall not murder.
7. You shall not commit adultery.
8. You shall not steal.
9. You shall not give false testimony.
10. You shall not covet.

— *Exodus 20:3–17*

"The secret things belong to the Lord our God, but the things revealed belong to us and to our children forever, that we may follow all the words of this law." — *Deuteronomy 29:29 (NIV)*

"A Boy Named Sue," artist: Johnny Cash. Songwriter: Shel Silverstein (Evil Eye Music, Inc.).

Johnny Cash found God later in life, and the gospel songs he performed continue to bless many people today. One beloved favorite is *"Were You There When They Crucified My Lord?"*

I will let this beautiful gospel song speak for itself:

"Were you there when they crucified my Lord?
Were you there when they crucified my Lord?
Oh, sometimes it causes me to tremble, tremble, tremble.
Were you there when they crucified my Lord?

Were you there when they took Him from the cross?
Were you there when they took Him from the cross?
Oh, sometimes it causes me to tremble, tremble, tremble.
Were you there when they took Him from the cross?

Were you there when they laid Him in the tomb?
Were you there when they laid Him in the tomb?
Oh, sometimes it causes me to tremble, tremble, tremble.
Were you there when they laid Him in the tomb?

Were you there when the stone was rolled away?
Were you there when the stone was rolled away?
Oh, sometimes it causes me to tremble, tremble, tremble.
Were you there when the stone was rolled away?"

"Were You There When They Crucified My Lord?" artist: Johnny Cash. Songwriter: Roy Venice (Music Chapel and Company, Inc.).

If you've never heard this powerful song, please make a point to do so—you will be greatly blessed.

"But I, when I am lifted up from the earth, will draw all men to Myself." — *John 12:32 (NIV)*

CHAPTER 5

King Solomon was the son of King David and Bathsheba. In 2 Chronicles, God appeared to Solomon and told him He would give him whatever he desired. Solomon asked God for wisdom so that he could lead his people in a way that would benefit everyone. Because of Solomon's genuine concern for the people, God not only granted him wisdom but also great wealth, riches, and fame, surpassing any king who had lived or who would ever live.

The book of 1 Kings tells us of Solomon's exceptional writing abilities. He composed about 3,000 proverbs and wrote 1,005 songs—the greatest of these being the *Song of Songs*. He was remarkably knowledgeable about plants, animals, birds, small creatures, and fish. Kings from all nations sent ambassadors just to listen to King Solomon's wisdom. His riches included vast quantities of gold, silver, gems, livestock, and properties. Solomon reigned from approximately 970 BC to 931 BC, and during this time, he received an estimated 25 tons of gold each year—for 39 years—a total of approximately 1,500 tons. In today's value, this would amount to billions of dollars. Indeed, no other man in history has ever been worth trillions.

(T.G. Pipher, Vocational College Teacher, Indiana Vocational Technology College)

In 1 Kings chapter 11, the Lord specifically warned Solomon not to marry foreign women. Yet, Solomon had 700 wives of royal birth and 300 concubines (secondary wives of inferior rank). One can't help but wonder how Solomon ever managed his extensive "honey-do" list! Unfortunately, it seems he attended to it far better than he should have, because over time, these foreign wives turned Solomon's heart away from God toward the worship of foreign idols. He even built shrines for these wives, where they burned incense and sacrificed to their gods. This became Solomon's downfall and a testimony to his own words:

> "There is not a righteous man on earth who does what is right and never sins." — *Ecclesiastes 7:20 (NIV)*

The books of Proverbs and Ecclesiastes, both authored by Solomon, are very much worth reading. Proverbs has 31 chapters—one for each day of the month—and Ecclesiastes has 12 chapters. Proverbs was written primarily to impart wisdom, whereas Ecclesiastes conveys that everything apart from God is empty and without meaning. Below is a brief sample of what the Holy Spirit wrote through Solomon:

From Proverbs:

> "Trust in the Lord with all your heart and lean not on your own understanding; in all your ways acknowledge Him,

"The Lord is my light and my salvation—whom shall I fear?

The Lord is the stronghold of my life—of whom shall I be afraid?"

— Psalm 27:1 (NIV)

As you read and study Scripture, you will find yourself adding to your list of mantras—words of comfort and strength you'll include in your daily conversations with God.

"Be joyful always; pray continually;

Give thanks in all circumstances,

For this is God's will for you in Christ Jesus."

— 1 Thessalonians 5:16–18 (NIV)

The Heartbreak of Abortion

Abortion has spread across America like an evil plague. Millions of innocent babies have been murdered—stolen from their mothers' wombs. The practice has evolved to include both surgical and chemical abortions. Both are invasive procedures, and both result in pain—for the baby and, often, the mother. Unless the surgical abortion is botched, both methods always end with the death of the baby—and tragically, many times, the death or long-term physical damage of the mother as well.

If the procedure is mishandled and the baby is born alive, the most horrific part may follow: as heartbreaking as it is, the cries of the newborn are ignored. The baby is set aside and left to die—completely helpless and utterly alone.

A woman who has had an abortion may experience guilt and deep psychological anguish that lasts for years. Abortion is a no-win situation for everyone involved—except for the ones performing and arranging the procedures. Much money is made in the abortion industry, both from surgical and chemical means.

What about the Christian perspective on abortion? How should a believer in Jesus Christ feel about this practice? Perhaps approaching this topic from the viewpoint of our Lord and Savior might help shift the mindset of those on the fence.

Imagine this:

The baby boy felt nothing but safety, warmth, and nourishment. Snuggled within his mother's womb, he was in a haven—free from injury or harm. As the days passed, his heartbeat grew stronger. His little movements became more pronounced. He began sucking his thumb as he continued his journey from conception to birth.

His tiny hands and fingers pressed against the womb in movements only he could make—movements that, over time, formed unique fingerprints that would identify him for the rest of his life.

Though he could not fully comprehend his existence, he instinctively knew that a great adventure awaited. His spirit was at peace within the tranquil world God had prepared for him.

Then, one day, something foreign intruded into his perfect world. At first, it was distant and barely noticeable. But then it grew stronger. The baby boy experienced a concept unknown to his world: pain.

Pain turned to confusion. Confusion to fear. He instinctively wanted to flee—but he could not. He could not fight. He could not run. He could only endure the pain until, mercifully, it ended.

The final emotion he felt in his mother's womb was betrayal. Then came darkness.

But the soul of the baby boy was not lost. It became aware of a presence—warmth, peace, and overwhelming love. The memory of his brief, horrific experience faded and was gone—never to torment him again.

Jesus reached down and gently picked up the soul of the aborted baby boy. Holding him close, Jesus spiritually conveyed His never-ending love for this helpless little one. After several moments, He turned toward a waiting angel and, with great tenderness, placed the soul of the aborted baby into the angel's arms.

The angel saw the eyes of his Master glisten with tears—tears that reflected the sorrow and holy grief over the total disrespect shown toward the sanctity of God-given life. Yet, even in sorrow, there was overwhelming love. The soul of the aborted baby boy would now be lovingly cared for as he grew to a place of spiritual maturity and eternal peace in Heaven.

As the angel carried him along, the spiritual mind of the child was filled with the Word of God:

> "The Lord will fulfill His purpose for me;
> Your love, O Lord, endures forever."
>
> — *Psalm 138:8 (NIV)*

> "For You created my inmost being;
> You knit me together in my mother's womb.
> I praise You because I am fearfully and wonderfully made."
>
> — *Psalm 139:13–14 (NIV)*

It is important to understand that if the mother of the aborted child repents of her sin and accepts Jesus Christ as her Savior and Lord, she will be reunited with that precious soul in heaven at the time of her physical death. God's mercy is great, and His grace covers even this.

The term "abortion" is not a modern invention. As early as the first century, moral teachings condemned the practice. In one of the earliest Christian ethics books, *The Didache*, we read:

> "You shall not murder a child by abortion, nor kill that which is begotten."

This book is considered part of the *Patristic* writings—early Christian literature believed to have been written by disciples of the Apostles themselves.

The Authority of God's Word

The Holy Bible was divinely authored by God, the Holy Spirit, using human writers of His choosing. It is completely infallible and free from error. However, throughout history, men have distorted its meaning by using human intellect rather than divine revelation.

One such example is the belief system held by Jehovah's Witnesses, a religious sect founded in the late 19th century. While the word "Jehovah" is indeed another name for God, Jehovah's Witnesses hold doctrines that contradict core biblical truths.

Jehovah's Witnesses believe in the imminent destruction of the world's wicked systems and the establishment of a theocracy—rule by God. While the concept of God's rule is true in Scripture, their interpretation is deeply flawed in several ways:

- **They incorrectly teach that the archangel Michael is the "Word" referred to in John 1:1–5,** thereby excluding Jesus, the Son of God, from His place as the second person of the Holy Trinity.
- **They teach that Jesus is the "wisdom" described in Proverbs 8,** implying He is a created being, rather than co-eternal and co-equal with the Father.
- **They deny the immortality of the soul,** teaching that most people cease to exist entirely at death.
- **They deny the existence of hell** as traditionally portrayed, claiming that death is simply the opposite of life, not a gateway to judgment.

- **They do not believe in the personhood of the Holy Spirit**, rejecting Him as a divine being and instead describing Him as merely a force or power.

These teachings are examples of how Scripture can be twisted when removed from the context of the full counsel of God. The Bible must be read with spiritual discernment, guided by the Holy Spirit, and not through the lens of man's logic alone.

Based on Revelation 14:1–4, Jehovah's Witnesses teach that exactly 144,000 of the most faithful believers will go to heaven to rule with the prophet Christ. Therefore, the only hope for the average Witness is to live with the hope that they might be counted among this elite number. The rest, they believe, will live on a restored Earth, while only the 144,000 enjoy a heavenly reward.

But this doctrine, like many others within the Jehovah's Witnesses' teachings, distorts the nature of God the Father, God the Son, and God the Holy Spirit. It denies essential truths of Scripture and follows a blasphemous belief system that leads to spiritual destruction. They reject the deity of Christ, reinterpret foundational texts, and deny the personhood and divinity of the Holy Spirit.

The Mormon Religion: Another Gospel

The religious sect known as the Mormons—or The Church of Jesus Christ of Latter-day Saints—also deviates dramatically from Biblical Christianity.

Mormons believe that God the Father, God the Son, and God the Holy Spirit are three separate gods among many other gods. They teach that humans are not saved by grace alone but may ascend to godhood themselves by keeping moral laws and participating in religious rituals. This doctrine rejects the finished work of Christ on the cross.

Mormons believe the Christian church fell into apostasy—a complete abandonment of the true faith—and that Joseph Smith was chosen by God to restore the true gospel. Mormons hold the Book of Mormon as sacred scripture, claiming it is a record of ancient people in the Americas, abridged by the prophet Mormon and translated by Joseph Smith from golden plates between 1827 and 1830.

Among their early practices was polygamy—the marriage of one man to multiple women. While polygamy is illegal in the United States, it has been decriminalized in Utah, a state with a high Mormon population.

There is a vast divide between Biblical Christianity and Mormonism in their views on:

- The nature of God
- The deification of believers
- The deity of Christ
- The Trinity
- Salvation by grace through faith

The Mormons and Jehovah's Witnesses walk hand-in-hand on a road paved with false teachings—a road that leads to eternal separation from God.

My prayer is that many will recognize the impurity of these doctrines, repent, and turn to the only true source of salvation—Jesus Christ.

> "I and the Father are one."
>
> — *John 10:30 (NIV)*

> "I am the Way and the Truth and the Life. No one comes to the Father except through Me."
>
> — *John 14:6 (NIV)*

Let God Be True

When weighing the beliefs of men, consider the truth of God's Word:

> "Let God be true, and every man a liar. As it is written:
>
> 'So that you may be proved right when you speak and prevail when you judge.'"
>
> — *Romans 3:4 (NIV)*

In regard to the Holy Spirit, Jesus promised this to His followers:

> "If you love Me, you will obey what I command.
>
> And I will ask the Father, and He will give you another Counselor to be with you forever—
>
> The Spirit of Truth.

The world cannot accept Him, because it neither sees
Him nor knows Him.

But you know Him, for He lives with you and will be in
you."

— John 14:15–17 (NIV)

If Jesus was crucified on Friday and resurrected on the third
day following, using modern time of 24-hour days, His rising
from the dead would've been on Monday. Does this mean that
the Bible is in error? For it says He was raised to life on Sunday. The reason for the difference is the length of the ancient
Hebrew day, which was 12 hours. On the day of the crucifixion, Good Friday would've been on the cycle of Friday starting at midnight. Those were the 12 hours during which Peter
denied Jesus three times before the rooster crowed.

"I tell you the truth," Jesus answered, "this very night,
before the rooster crows, you will disown Me three
times."

— Matthew 26:34 (NIV)

To which Peter declared:

"Even if I have to die with you, I will never disown you."
— Matthew 26:35 (NIV)

After Jesus was arrested and taken away, Peter—being afraid
for his own life—followed at a distance and sat in the court-

yard where Jesus had been taken. There, he was accused three times of being one of the disciples of Jesus. The third time this happened, he began to curse and swore to the people he was among that he didn't know Jesus. Instantly, a rooster crowed, and Peter remembered what Jesus had said. He went outside the courtyard and wept bitterly.

Saturday would have begun at noon, following the crucifixion. On this day, the chief priests and Pharisees went to Pilate and asked that the tomb where the body of Jesus had been placed be made secure and guards posted. They did this for fear the disciples would steal the body and claim Jesus had risen from the dead. Permission was granted, the tomb was sealed, and guards were posted.

Sunday would've begun at midnight and lasted until noon. Early on this morning, Mary Magdalene went to the tomb and saw the large stone had been removed and the tomb was empty. She hurried and told Peter and John what she had discovered. Full of excitement, the two men ran to the tomb. When they went into the empty tomb, they found the linen strips that had been wrapped around the body of Jesus, as well as the cloth that had been placed around His head, lying flat and undisturbed—as if the body had mysteriously disappeared.

Though they had not fully understood that Jesus would rise from the dead, this made them realize He had indeed been resurrected.

CHAPTER 7

Down a rarely used hallway of my mind is a locked closet door. Inside the closet, at the very bottom of a stack of rarely used thoughts, lies the unthinkable sin. I don't remember when I became aware of this sin. It might have been through an article I read about some infamous serial killer, or it could be that within all of us lies the entirety of every sin that can be committed. Thankfully, most never come to pass. Whatever the reason, I have kept it well suppressed, for after all, it is the unthinkable sin.

I suppose it surfaced because of the evilness in today's world—an evilness that is growing day by day. I am sure many would agree that it is truly difficult to listen to the daily news.

So, what am I talking about? What is this horrible sin we must not even think about? On your electronic device, **Google:** What is the term for having sex with a human corpse? "Necrophilia" appears, which is a Greek word meaning *philia* (attraction to love) and *nekros* (dead body). These terms involve sexual attraction to a dead body. Necrophilia is an obsession with erotic interest in a corpse.

This is a depravity not unique to any one modern culture. On occasion, even members of the feminine sex have been drawn to this practice. However, only Islam contains scriptures, commentary, and decrees permitting the macabre practice.

As with most of Islam's problematic teachings, necrophilia is traceable to Muhammad. Muhammad was an Arab religious, social, and political leader. At the age of 40, he supposedly had revelations from Allah that became the basis for the Quran and the foundation of Islam.

The ghastly ugliness of necrophilia cannot be described in human terms. Satan himself and the demons that follow him participate through demonic possession, as the depths of their loathing for God and the human race He created are fully displayed. The holy angels in heaven look on in disdain as they watch the ravenous display of contempt and scorn culminate in the final climactic stage. This is the bitter-tasting icing on the unholy cake.

While this is truly the unthinkable sin, it is not unforgivable. If the one who allowed demonic possession to occur prayed for deliverance and lay at the foot of the cross, imploring forgiveness, the blood of Jesus would cleanse them.

It would be difficult for an atheist to deflect questions regarding the unthinkable sin. What person in their right mind would say there is nothing wrong with this deplorable act? However, if one truly did not believe in God and His morals, there would be nothing wrong with necrophilia. Without God, one cannot pick and choose, for without God, anything goes.

All this is relatable to God's calling of Abram. The Lord told Abram to leave his country, his people, and his father's household and to go to the land of Canaan, which would be shown to him. God said to Abram:

> "I will make you into a great nation, and I will bless you;
>
> I will make your name great, and you will be a blessing.
>
> I will bless those who bless you,
>
> And whoever curses you I will curse;
>
> And all peoples on earth will be blessed through you."
>
> — *Genesis 12:2–3 (NIV)*

At the time of Abram's arrival, the Canaanites were in the land. The Lord appeared to Abram and told him:

> "To your offspring I will give this land."
>
> — *Genesis 12:7 (NIV)*

This was more than 400 years before God's commandments were given to Moses. Therefore, there was no way to judge the quality of Abram's morals. However, because Abram believed what God told him, God considered him to be righteous.

> "Abram believed the Lord, and He credited it to him as righteousness."
>
> — *Genesis 15:6 (NIV)*

"If, in fact, Abram was justified by works, he had something to boast about—but not before God. What does Scripture say? 'Abraham believed God, and it was credited to him as righteousness.'"

— *Romans 4:2–3 (NIV)*

Abram's wife, Sarai, had borne no children. Because of this, she told Abram to sleep with her Egyptian maidservant, Hagar, with the hope that she could build a family through her. Abram agreed to this, and through Hagar, Abram's first son, Ishmael, was born.

God told Hagar:

"You are now with child, and you will have a son.

You shall name him Ishmael,

For the Lord has heard of your misery.

He will be a wild donkey of a man;

His hand will be against everyone,

And everyone's hand against him,

And he will live in hostility toward all his brothers."

— *Genesis 16:11–12 (NIV)*

An Ishmaelite is a member of a biblical people descended from Ishmael, who is regarded by Muslims as a progenitor of the Arab people. In Genesis 25, the Bible says that Ishmael lived to the age of 137 years. His Arab descendants lived then, and continue to do so today, in hostility toward their Jewish brothers.

The reality of a two-state solution will never come about in Israel. The only solution radical Islam is interested in is the total destruction of Israel and God's chosen people.

God kept His promise to Abram and Sarai, as she became pregnant and bore a son to Abram. Abram was 100 years old when his son, whom he named Isaac, was born. Before the birth of Isaac, God gave to Abraham the covenant of circumcision. At that time, God told Abraham he would be known as Abraham, and his wife Sarai would be called Sarah.

At age 40, Isaac married Rebekah, and she became pregnant and gave birth to twin boys. The first twin to be born was named Esau, and the second twin was named Jacob. It was customary for a birthright to be given to the firstborn son. This included a double portion of the family inheritance and the honor of becoming the family leader. The oldest son could sell or give away his birthright, but if he did, all benefits given by the birthright would be lost. Esau showed no interest in the benefits he would receive by keeping his birthright.

"The Lord said to Rebekah, 'Two nations are in your womb, and two peoples from within you will be separated; one people will be stronger than the other, and the older will serve the younger.'" —Genesis 25:23 (NIV)

The boys grew up, and Esau became a skillful hunter, a man of the open country, while Jacob was a quiet man, staying among the tents. Isaac, who had a taste for wild game, loved Esau, but Rebekah loved Jacob.

Once, when Jacob was cooking some stew, Esau came in from the open country, famished. He said to Jacob, "Quick, let me have some of that red stew! I'm famished!" —Genesis 25:27–30 (NIV)

> Jacob replied, "First sell me your birthright."
>
> "Look, I'm about to die," Esau said. "What good is the birthright to me?"
>
> But Jacob said, "Swear to me first."
>
> So he swore an oath to him, selling his birthright to Jacob. Then Jacob gave Esau some bread and some lentil stew. He ate and drank, and then got up and left.
>
> So Esau despised his birthright.
>
> —*Genesis 25:31–34 (NIV)*

After this, the Jewish forefather Jacob was renamed *Israel* by the Lord God. So it came to pass that the son of Isaac and Rebekah, and grandson of the patriarch Abraham, fathered twelve sons. They are the ancestors of the twelve tribes of Israel.

CHAPTER 8

Syphilis is a sexually transmitted infection caused by a bacterial infection that enters through broken skin or mucous membranes. For the most part, this is a medical condition that had been brought under suppression but has made a frightening comeback over the past few years.

Men suffer sores at the original site of infection, usually on or around the genitals, around the anus or in the rectum, or in or around the mouth.

Women suffer small, round, firm sores at the entrance site of the body, such as the vulva, vagina, tongue, and lips. The infection may also be inside the vagina or rectum.

Syphilis is a chronic infectious disease that can affect almost any body organ, including the skin, brain, and nervous tissue. While penicillin shots administered to prostitutes on a regular basis had been keeping syphilis at bay, the rise in this deadly disease is due to casual, unnatural, and uninhibited sex within the general public. There is a price to pay when God's plan for sex—only between a married man and woman—is not followed.

If a relative invited you to their same-sex wedding, would you attend in order to show love and support for that relative? If you are a Christian, you should not. The marriage would be contrary to God's law, for marriage is to be between one man and one woman for life.

If, at a future date after the wedding, you had a family gathering, should you invite that relative, or would you consider them to no longer be part of the family? Of course, you should invite that relative—especially because you are a Christian.

Should you invite the same-sex partner to the family gathering? Of course, you should, for the new command given to us by the Lord Jesus has no exclusions:

> "A new command I give you: Love one another. As I have loved you, so you must love one another. By this all men will know that you are My disciples, if you love one another."

> —John 13:34–35 NIV

In actuality, even though this particular sin is an abomination to the Lord, the only difference between them and you is the fact that you have repented for your sins and have accepted Jesus as your Lord and Savior. Even though God no longer sees your sins—for they were laid on Jesus at the cross—the same-sex couple is as precious to Him as you are.

The only stipulation you should make to the same-sex couple is that there is to be no unnatural affection shown at your home or any other place to which you have invited them. The point is to try and draw them to God by the love you have shown—and not to be drawn away from Him.

The same train of thought should be followed in any Bible-believing church. No one should be turned away from an opportunity to find God. The pastor and elders should counsel same-sex couples and any known homosexuals regarding what their conduct must be while on church property. During sermons, the pastor must not preach around the topic of homosexuality, but instead preach the true Word of God. Same-sex couples and known homosexuals should receive sincere, godly fellowship at church and while attending any church-sponsored activity.

What brings joy to the eyes of the Lord? A husband and wife holding hands as they walk together, enjoying the beauty of nature. Parents walking with their children, holding their hands in a protective and loving manner. A man and woman holding hands during godly courtship, walking side by side and enjoying one another's presence.

Humanity wants to rule with God—or in place of God. The believer, however, wants to be ruled by God and experience His perfect peace, harmony, and joy. The simplicity of receiving God cannot be denied. Sadly, rebellious pride often prevents this balance. However, God made everything, and anything within that everything belongs to Him.

Saint Anselm of Canterbury was quoted as saying, *"God is that than which no greater can be conceived."*

It is amazing that those who rant against God cannot do so without using foul language. It is as if they twist the dagger after making the strike—and then spit in the face of the One who made them.

"To fear the Lord is to hate evil; I hate pride and arrogance, evil behavior and perverse speech." —Proverbs 8:13, NIV

What are some facts that give evidence of creation instead of evolution? While they are endless in number, a good place to start is the fact of the ability to read—and of course, the ability to read would be useless without first having the ability to write the things we read.

Why is it that human beings are the only creatures on Earth with the ability to write and read? Could it be that being born in the image of God is a reference to intelligence?

"Then God said, 'Let us make man in Our image, in Our likeness, and let them rule over the fish of the sea and the birds of the air, over the livestock, over all the Earth, and over all the creatures that move along the ground.'" —Genesis 1:26, NIV

Because of sin, things didn't turn out the way God intended. But because of our God-given intelligence comes everything we know and understand up to the current time in human history. To have the mental power concerned with forming conclusions and judgment is given only to humanity.

To be made holy is to be set apart and committed to God. The reasons for which something exists or is done are purposeful, God-given reasons. While the world's truth changes as needed—being related to current circumstances and opinions—God's truth is absolute.

God's foundation for all things is love. The main driving force behind creation was love.

"If I speak in the tongues of men and of angels, but have not love, I am only a resounding gong or a clanging cymbal. If I have the gift of prophecy and can fathom all mysteries and all knowledge, and if I have a faith that can move mountains, but have not love, I am nothing. If I give all I possess to the poor and surrender my body to the flames, but have not love, I gain nothing." —1 Corinthians 13:1–3, NIV

"Love is patient, love is kind. It does not envy, it does not boast, it is not proud. It is not rude, it is not self-seeking, it is not easily angered, it keeps no record of wrongs. Love does not delight in evil but rejoices with the truth. It always protects, always trusts, always hopes, always perseveres." —1 Corinthians 13:4–7, NIV

"Now we see but a poor reflection as in a mirror; then we shall see face to face. Now I know in part; then I shall know fully, even as I am fully known. And now these three remain: faith, hope, and love. But the greatest of these is love." —1 Corinthians 13:12–13, NIV

When the chips are down, those of the Christian faith usually receive trust and respect from the general secular public. For example, take a non-believing young married couple with a small child. Imagine they took the wrong exit from a busy freeway and found themselves on the wrong side of town. As luck would have it, at the worst possible location, the car broke down, coasting to the side of the road and stopping against the curb.

The young couple surveyed their surroundings as they apprehensively watched the approaching darkness. Down the street on one side was a church. A sign in front of the building read: *Church of the Living God – Everyone Welcome.* A little farther along, on the opposite side of the street, was a brightly lit, flashing sign that read: *Hells Angels Hideaway – Nude Dancing Girls and Much More.*

To whom do you believe the young couple and their child would go to obtain assistance?

It should be obvious. They would seek the comfort and safety of the Bible-believing church. In a situation such as this, those with a sound mind would naturally be drawn to the ones who exhibit the fruit of the Spirit:

> "But the fruit of the Spirit is love, joy, peace, patience, kindness, goodness, faithfulness, gentleness, and self-control. Against such things there is no law."
>
> —Galatians 5:22–24, NIV

The purpose of the law is to make us conscious of sin. There is no law needed when no law is broken.

The fruit of the Spirit comes about by born-again believers having the Spirit of God living within them:

"If you love Me, you will obey what I command. And I will ask the Father, and He will give you another Counselor to be with you forever— the Spirit of truth. The world cannot accept Him, because it neither sees Him nor knows Him. But you know Him, for He lives with you and will be in you."

—John 14:15–17, NIV

Sadly, in today's world, there are those who openly seek the fruit of the flesh. These people want nothing to do with God and His morality. Thinking they will find happiness and fulfillment, they find the opposite—only heartbreak and sorrow.

"The acts of the sinful nature are obvious: sexual immorality, impurity and debauchery; idolatry and witchcraft; hatred, discord, jealousy, fits of rage, selfish ambition, dissensions, factions and envy; drunkenness, orgies, and the like. I warn you, as I did before, that those who live like this will not inherit the kingdom of God." —Galatians 5:19–21, NIV

"If a prophet, or one who foretells by dreams, appears among you and announces to you a miraculous sign or wonder, and if the sign or wonder of which he has spoken takes place, and he says, 'Let us follow other gods' (gods you have not known), 'and let us worship them,' you must not listen to the words of that prophet or dreamer. The Lord your God is testing you to find out whether you love Him with all your heart and with all your soul. It is the Lord your God you must follow, and Him you must revere. Keep His commandments and obey Him; serve Him and hold fast to Him." —Deuteronomy 13:1–4, NIV

"The heart is deceitful above all things and beyond cure. Who can understand it?

'I the Lord search the heart and examine the mind, to reward a man according to his conduct, according to what his deeds deserve.'" —Jeremiah 17:9–10, NIV

Although the heart is filled with evil, a wonderful change occurs when one accepts Christ and is filled with the Holy Spirit. The evilness of the carnal heart is replaced by God's goodness.

"The man without the Spirit does not accept the things that come from the Spirit of God, for they are foolishness to him, and he cannot understand them, because they are spiritually discerned." —1 Corinthians 2:14, NIV

CHAPTER 9

In *Psalm 22*, David gave an accurate description of the suffering Jesus would experience on the cross. The crucifixion of Jesus was hundreds of years after this psalm was written:

"My God, My God, why have You forsaken Me?

Why are You so far from saving Me,

so far from the words of My groaning?

O My God, I cry out by day, but You do not answer,

by night, and am not silent.

Yet You are enthroned as the Holy One;

You are the praise of Israel.

In You our fathers put their trust;

they trusted and You delivered them.

They cried to You and were saved;

In You they trusted and were not disappointed.

But I am a worm and not a man,

scorned by men and despised by the people.

All who see Me mock Me;

they hurl insults, shaking their heads:
'He trusts in the Lord; let the Lord rescue Him.
Let Him deliver Him, since He delights in Him.'

Yet You brought Me out of the womb;
You made Me trust in You
even at My mother's breast.
From birth I was cast upon You;
from My mother's womb You have been My God.
Do not be far from Me,
for trouble is near and there is no one to help.

Many bulls surround Me;
strong bulls of Bashan encircle Me.
Roaring lions tearing their prey
open their mouths wide against Me.
I am poured out like water,
and all My bones are out of joint.
My heart has turned to wax;
it has melted away within Me.
My strength is dried up like a potsherd,
and My tongue sticks to the roof of My mouth;
You lay Me in the dust of death.
Dogs have surrounded Me;

a band of evil men has encircled Me,
they have pierced My hands and My feet.
I can count all My bones;
people stare and gloat over Me.
They divide My garments among them
and cast lots for My clothing."

—Psalms 22:1–18, NIV

"All that was destroyed will be restored. All creation will be made whole again—beauty instead of ashes.

"The Spirit of the Sovereign Lord is on Me,
because the Lord has anointed Me
to preach good news to the poor.
He has sent Me to bind up the brokenhearted,
to proclaim freedom for the captives
and release from darkness for the prisoners,
to proclaim the year of the Lord's favor
and the day of vengeance of our God,
to comfort all who mourn,
and provide for those who grieve in Zion—
to bestow on them a crown of beauty instead of ashes,
the oil of gladness instead of mourning,
and a garment of praise instead of a spirit of despair.

They will be called oaks of righteousness,
a planting of the Lord
for the display of His splendor."

—Isaiah 61:1–3, NIV

"They will rebuild the ancient ruins
and restore the places long devastated;
they will renew the ruined cities
that have been devastated for generations.
Aliens will shepherd your flocks;
foreigners will work your fields and vineyards.
And you will be called priests of the Lord,
you will be named ministers of our God.
You will feed on the wealth of nations,
and in their riches you will boast.

Instead of their shame,
My people will receive a double portion,
and instead of disgrace
they will rejoice in their inheritance;
and so they will inherit a double portion in their land,
and everlasting joy will be theirs.

For I, the Lord, love justice;
I hate robbery and iniquity.
In My faithfulness I will reward them
and make an everlasting covenant with them.
Their descendants will be known among the nations,
and their offspring among the peoples.
All who see them will acknowledge
that they are a people the Lord has blessed."

I delight greatly in the Lord;
My soul rejoices in My God.
For He has clothed Me with garments of salvation
and arrayed Me in a robe of righteousness,
as a bridegroom adorns His head like a priest,
and as a bride adorns herself with her jewels.
For as the soil makes the sprout come up
and a garden causes seeds to grow,
so the Sovereign Lord will make righteousness and praise
spring up before all nations.

—Isaiah 61:1–11, NIV**

While the birth of Jesus is celebrated on December 25, the Bible tells us December was not the month of His birth.

The birth of Jesus was foretold:

"In the sixth month, God sent the angel Gabriel to Nazareth, a town in Galilee, to a virgin pledged to be married to a man named Joseph, a descendant of David. The virgin's name was Mary. The angel went to her and said, 'Greetings, you who are highly favored! The Lord is with you."

—Luke 1:26–28, NIV

Mary was greatly troubled at his words and wondered what kind of greeting this might be. But the angel said to her, "Do not be afraid, Mary; you have found favor with God. You will be with child and give birth to a Son, and you are to give Him the name Jesus. He will be great and will be called the Son of the Most High."

—Luke 1:29–32, NIV

"How will this be," Mary asked the angel, "since I am a virgin?"

The angel answered, "The Holy Spirit will come upon you, and the power of the Most High will overshadow you. So the Holy One to be born will be called the Son of God. Even Elizabeth, your relative, is going to have a child in her old age, and she who was said to be barren is in her sixth month. For nothing is impossible with God."

—Luke 1:34–35, NIV

The baby Elizabeth was going to have was John the Baptist, the prophet who was to go before Jesus to announce Him and to prepare the way for Him.

Shortly after the angel's visit, Mary hurried to Elizabeth's home. When Elizabeth heard Mary's greeting, the baby leaped in her womb, and Elizabeth was filled with the Holy Spirit. In a loud voice, she exclaimed,

> "Blessed are you among women, and blessed is the child you will bear!"
>
> —Luke 1:41–42, NIV

By this, it is shown that Mary was already with child when she visited Elizabeth. Since this occurred in the sixth month (June), the birth of Jesus would have been in March.

At the birth of baby Jesus, shepherds were living in the fields, watching over their flocks at night. An angel appeared to them, and they were very frightened. But the angel said to them,

"Do not be afraid. I bring you good news of great joy that will be for all the people. Today in the town of David, a Savior has been born to you; He is Christ the Lord. This will be a sign to you: you will find a baby wrapped in cloths and lying in a manger."

Suddenly a great company of the heavenly host appeared with the angel, praising God and saying,

"Glory to God in the highest, and on earth peace to men on whom His favor rests."

—Luke 2:10–14, NIV

When the angels had left them and gone into heaven, the shepherds said to one another,

"Let's go to Bethlehem and see this thing that has happened, which the Lord has told us about."

So they hurried off and found Mary and Joseph, and the baby, who was lying in the manger.

When they had seen Him, they spread the word concerning what had been told them about this child, and all who heard it were amazed at what the shepherds said to them." —Luke 2:15–18, NIV

After the birth of Jesus, Magi from the East saw His star and eventually traveled to Bethlehem to worship Him:

"But you, Bethlehem, in the land of Judah, are by no means least among the rulers of Judah; for out of you will come a ruler who will be the shepherd of My people Israel."

—Matthew 2:6, NIV

While the Magi were wealthy, learned men with great authority, they did not have the convenience of loading treasures into a jet cargo bay and flying off to Bethlehem to worship the Lord Jesus Christ. On the contrary, they traveled in a caravan consisting of many people, provisions, and security. Because of the time needed to arrange and organize their journey—and the miles they would travel—it took several years to reach their destination.

The caravan would have been an imposing sight as it slowly made its way across the desert, accompanied by a large security force that displayed power sufficient to intimidate any would-be attackers.

When the Magi arrived, Jesus was living in a house with His mother, Mary, and it is thought that He was six or seven years old.

"After they had heard the king, they went on their way, and the star they had seen in the East went ahead of them until it stopped over the place where the child was. When they saw the star, they were overjoyed.

On coming to the house, they saw the child with His mother Mary, and they bowed down and worshiped Him. Then they opened their treasures and presented Him with gifts of gold and incense." —Matthew 2:9–11, NIV

The Baptism of Jesus

In those days, John the Baptist came preaching in the desert of Judea and saying, "Repent, for the kingdom of heaven is near." This is He who was spoken of through the prophet Isaiah:

"A voice of one calling in the desert,

'Prepare the way for the Lord,

make straight paths for Him.'"

—Matthew 3:1–3, NIV

Then Jesus came from Galilee to the Jordan to be baptized by John. But John tried to deter Him, saying, "I need to be baptized by You, and do You come to me?"

Jesus replied, "Let it be so now; it is proper for us to do this to fulfill all righteousness." Then John consented.

As soon as Jesus was baptized, He went up out of the water. At that moment, heaven was opened, and He saw the Spirit of God descending like a dove and lighting on Him. And a voice from heaven said,

"This is my Son, whom I love; with Him I am well pleased."

—Matthew 3:13–17, NIV

When Jesus was baptized by John, we have a clear example of the Holy Trinity working together: the voice from heaven was God the Father; the dove descending from the sky was God the Holy Spirit; and, of course, Jesus is God the Son.

What is the purpose of baptism? Is it something essential in order to be born again?

Baptism has nothing to do with one's salvation. The only pathway to heaven is through the blood of Jesus Christ:

"I am the Way and the Truth and the Life. No one comes to the Father except through Me."

—John 14:6, NIV

Neither this nor any other biblical passage suggests baptism is necessary for salvation.

Water baptism is an act of acknowledgment that symbolizes the death, burial, and resurrection of a believer in Christ. Being laid back and immersed in water represents burial, and being raised up from the water represents resurrection to eternal life. Water baptism is also a statement that professes faith in Christ after being born again.

If an adult is baptized without asking for the forgiveness of their sins, they are not saved. If one was baptized as an infant or a child but never asked for forgiveness of their sins, they are not saved. One must acknowledge their belief in Jesus and ask for forgiveness of sins in order to enter the Kingdom of God.

Two criminals were crucified along with Jesus, one hanging on each side of Him. One of the criminals who hung there hurled insults at Him:

"Aren't You the Christ? Save yourself and us!"

But the other criminal rebuked Him:

"Don't you fear God," he said, "since you are under the same sentence? We are punished justly, for we are getting what our deeds deserve. But this Man has done nothing wrong." Then he said,

"Jesus, remember me when You come into Your kingdom."

Jesus answered him:

"I tell you the truth, today you will be with Me in paradise."

—Luke 23:39–43, NIV

The fact that this criminal could not be baptized had nothing to do with his salvation. Whether being immersed in it or sprinkled by it, water will not wash away our sins. Only the precious blood of Jesus can accomplish this.

CHAPTER 10

In my mind's eye, I and some others witnessed a unique game of poker. The gameplay was one hand of five-card draw—winner takes all. The uniqueness came from the fact that this poker game was being played between the devil and a born-again believer.

The hand had progressed to the point where the devil had all five of his cards face up on the table. The believer had four cards face up, and the dealer was ready to turn the fifth.

From the beginning of the game, the devil had unceasingly harassed the believer, living up to his nickname: *the accuser.* Accusations flew like leaves in a whirlwind. Trash talk came rapid-fire, particularly about the believer's past struggles to acknowledge God and submit to His sovereignty before redemption. The devil gleefully brought to light the believer's previous rejection of God's moral laws and a life filled with lying, drunkenness, and immoral sexual encounters.

"Do you really believe God has forgiven you for these things?" the devil hissed. "You're very foolish if you do. I have your reservation to Hell neatly tucked away in my hip pocket—I'll show it to you shortly. You know you don't have a chance to beat me."

And so the taunting continued.

Indeed, the devil had an excellent hand. Four nines and the jack of spades lay before him—a formidable combination. The believer had the ten, jack, queen, and king of hearts on the table. Since the devil held all four nines, the believer's hand was not open at both ends. Still, all was not lost.

There was a slim chance.

If the believer was dealt the ace of hearts, it would complete a royal flush—the highest possible hand in poker. Alternatively, the ace of diamonds, ace of clubs, or ace of spades would give him a straight flush—still enough to beat the devil's four of a kind.

With 43 cards left in play, it was a long shot—but not impossible.

The dealer slowly turned over the believer's final card.

When the devil saw what lay before the believer, his rage was instant and unmistakable. The onlookers watching the card game instinctively took a step back, fearing their presence might provoke him further.

Pouring forth vile exclamations, the devil rose from his chair, turned, and walked away from the circle of spectators. After taking several steps, he disappeared—vanished into thin air—but his furious cursing could still be heard for several moments.

Then... silence.

Slowly, the onlookers walked to the table where the believer sat. They wanted to see whether it was a royal flush or a straight flush that had beaten the devil's four of a kind. But when they saw the fifth card, they gasped in astonishment—for the believer had not drawn any of the aces he needed.

The "ace in the hole" for the born-again believer was a picture of the cross.

The one who was above the other angels in rank before his fall understands the truth of Scripture. That is the reason for his fury.

Then I heard a loud voice in heaven say: "Now have come the salvation and the power and the kingdom of our God, and the authority of His Christ. For the accuser of our brothers, who accuses them before our God day and night, has been hurled down." —Revelation 12:10 (NIV)

He is filled with fury, because he knows that his time is short. —Revelation 12:12 (NIV)

Why is My language not clear to you? Because you are unable to hear what I say. You belong to your father, the devil, and you want to carry out your father's desire. He was a murderer from the beginning, not holding to the truth, for there is no truth in him. When he lies, he speaks his native language, for he is a liar and the father of lies. —John 8:43–44 (NIV)

Do not be deceived by the devil's lies. Amazing grace is for all who believe in Jesus Christ.

I realize I'm about to reach a point in life where I should expect to see changes associated with growing older. Now, understand—I'm not there yet—but I have provided a way to make things easier when that time arrives.

What I'm referring to is my special notebook.

I must admit, this was a stroke of pure genius shining forth. In this special notebook, I've written down everything I'll need in order to continue living a productive and meaningful life. In fact, I suspect loved ones and friends won't notice any change in my ability to function. They won't even see a small bump in the road.

I'll now reveal what I've done—and I certainly don't object if anyone wants to follow my lead.

In my special notebook, I've written the names, birthdates, and phone numbers of my children, grandchildren, and great-grandchildren. I've also jotted down information about their personal likes and dislikes. Being the concerned patriarch that I am, I included the names of their pets, whether dog or cat—and what's needed to spoil them properly with food, entertainment, and gifts.

On a more personal level, I've ensured my senior years will be safe and secure with just the stroke of a pen. I've listed the name, phone number, and address of my primary care physician—along with a note on whether or not I like him.

Thankfully, I don't require much medication, but the few I do take (along with my vitamins) are all documented. In the unlikely event of a serious memory lapse, I've even written down the model, color, and license plate number of my car. I've also included the emergency number—119—in case of a crisis. As an added precaution, I drew simple maps to the businesses I most frequently visit. I don't want any whispered conversations among relatives about whether it's time to take Grandpa's keys.

Speaking of keys, my special notebook contains the location of my spare car keys, as well as where I've hidden the extra house key in case I accidentally lock myself out. After all, I'm not as young as I used to be, and I hate the idea of having to climb through a window. Hopefully, any crook hanging around will also be an old guy with bad knees and no interest in scaling windows.

All in all, I believe I've solved the problem of growing old—thanks to all I've written and the diagrams I've drawn. It was certainly worth the time and effort I put into the project.

Now… if I could just remember where I put that darn special notebook.

"All men and women are like grass, and all their glory is like the flowers of the field. The grass withers, and the flowers fall, but the word of the Lord stands forever." 1 Peter 1:24–25 (NIV)

Everything in this life—possessions, accomplishments, and people—will fade away. Only God's will, word, and work are permanent.

If you've also lost your own special notebook, 911 is the correct number to call in the event of an emergency. The three-digit telephone number has been designated as a universal number throughout the United States to request emergency assistance. It is intended as a nationwide emergency telephone number and provides the public with fast and easy access to a Public Safety Answering Point (PSAP).

If you have information about an emergency situation currently happening in a state, county, or city other than the one you're in, the best option is to dial the 10-digit phone number for law enforcement in that specific community where assistance is needed.

When God made reference to people as sheep, it was not meant as a compliment. One meaning of the word "sheep" is a meek, unimaginative, or easily led person. It has been said that if one were to place a sheep next to a small boulder of approximately the same size, it would be difficult to determine which of the two had more intelligence.

"We all, like sheep, have gone astray, each of us has turned to his own way." Isaiah 53:6 (NIV)

Psalm 23, which is written in its entirety in another section of this book, reveals our troublesome dilemma in this regard. In this psalm, David writes from his own experience caring for sheep. He knew firsthand that sheep are completely dependent on the shepherd for provision, guidance, and protection.

In the same way, Jesus watches over, directs, and protects those who believe in Him.

With His rod and staff, Jesus nudges and prods His lost sheep in the right direction, motivating and impelling them to follow His will—not their own. In doing so, Jesus leads and guides those who belong to Him through the very dangerous *valley of the shadow of death*, which is in constant battle with born-again believers.

There are people in our daily lives who believe they must behave in a condescending manner—descending from their perceived position of superiority, rank, or dignity—in order to communicate in a way they believe others will understand. This might include a supervisor addressing an employee under their authority, a teacher speaking to a student, a religious leader addressing their congregation, and much more. This mindset is especially prevalent in politics, where there are those who rush to the front of the line—uninvited—to meet their own needs before quickly returning to the "important" task of saving the world.

The truth of the matter is, we all, in one way or another, have probably shown a condescending attitude. It may have been directed toward the person on the corner begging for money, or perhaps toward the young married couple whose husband couldn't seem to hold onto a job. There are countless reasons we might, in a self-righteous way, look down on another human being.

However, in God's reality, it is impossible to interact with another person in a truly condescending way, because regardless of one's stature, no one is above another when it comes to human dignity and the sanctity of life, whether rich or poor, king or beggar—all are alike.

Whether a college professor, often regarded as a teacher of the highest academic rank, or an elementary teacher of lower rank—in God's eyes, all are equal.

There is only one true Condescender—and that is our God. He voluntarily put aside His holy dignity and superiority and came down to our level in order to interact with His created beings.

> Oh, long and dark the stairs I trod
> With trembling feet to find my God,
> Gaining a foothold bit by bit,
> Then slipping back and losing it.
> Never progressing, striving still,
> With weakening grasp and faltering will,
> Bleeding to climb to God—while He
> Serenely smiled, not noting me.
>
> Then came a certain time when I
> Loosened my hold and fell thereby,
> Down to the lowest step. My fall—
> As if I had not climbed at all.
>
> Now when I lay despairing there,
> I heard a footfall on the stair.

On that same stair where I, afraid,

Faltered and fell and lowly layed dismayed

And lo when hope had ceased to be—

My God came down the stairs to me.

—Anonymous

CHAPTER 11

The star that is our sun is 93,000,000 miles from Earth. The speed of the light that comes from our sun—as well as from all the other suns throughout the universe—is 186,000 miles per second. There are billions of suns throughout the universe, and at the speed of light, it takes 8 minutes and 20 seconds for sunlight to reach the Earth. If the sun were to suddenly disappear, the population of Earth would not be aware of this tragic event for 8 minutes and 20 seconds.

Neptune is the farthest planet from Earth within our solar system. At its closest approach, Neptune is approximately 2,700,000,000 miles away. On a spacecraft traveling 50,000 miles per hour, it would take 2,250 days—or a little over six years—to reach Neptune.

A solar system is a sun together with all the planets and other bodies that revolve around it. A galaxy is a massive system of suns, billions of light-years apart from each other, held together by mutual gravitation and isolated from similar systems by vast regions of space.

The nearest exoplanet, Alpha Centauri Bb, is 4.24 light-years away. Given the physical limit of the speed of light, the absolute minimum travel time—even in the reference frame of the traveler—is 4.24 years. But achieving velocities even close to that of light is far beyond our current capabilities.

The universe is the totality of all known—or even supposed—solar systems, galaxies, and phenomena throughout space. This is also known as the cosmos.

While we cannot fully imagine the power that created all of this, the thoughtfulness behind its design is incredible. Not only did God position the Earth exactly 93 million miles from the sun—precisely the distance required to sustain life—but it seems, as an afterthought, He also gave us added benefits from the sun beyond just life-giving warmth.

From 93 million miles away, God delivers a special gift: vitamin D.

Vitamin D regulates many cellular functions. Its anti-inflammatory, antioxidant, and neuroprotective properties support immune health, muscle function, and brain cell activity. On a sunny day, the skin can generate 10,000 IU of vitamin D just from UV light exposure.

So, while enjoying a beautiful summer day under the sun God made just for us, we are also reaping valuable health benefits—benefits that are very difficult to explain through the theory of evolution.

There is a belief held by a certain class of people that the God of the Bible is no longer relevant in today's modern society.

They believe that through their wealth, power, and technology, they will discover the path to eternal life on their own—unendangered and self-sufficient—ultimately becoming gods in the process. These individuals completely reject the truth that there is one God and that the only way to Him is through His Son, Jesus Christ.

"I am the Way and the Truth and the Life. No one comes to the Father except through Me." —John 14:6–7, NIV

God has appointed each of us a specific time to depart from this physical realm, and there is nothing anyone can do to prevent or prolong it. Only God knows with certainty where every individual who has experienced human life and moved on to the spiritual realm now resides.

It is only by turning from our sins and accepting Jesus Christ that we are assured immortality.

"Who of you by worrying can add a single hour to his life? Since you cannot do this very little thing, why do you worry about the rest? Consider how the lilies grow. They do not labor or spin. Yet I tell you, not even Solomon in all his splendor was dressed like one of these. If that is how God clothes the grass of the field, which is here today and tomorrow is thrown into the fire, how much more will He clothe you—O you of little faith!" —Luke 12:25–28, NIV

Jesus emphasized the reality of the resurrection and eternal life. Even in the account of the burning bush, Moses revealed that the dead do indeed rise:

"But in the account of the bush, even Moses showed that the dead rise, for he calls the Lord 'the God of Abraham, and the God of Isaac, and the God of Jacob.' He is not the God of the dead, but of the living, for to Him all are alive." —Luke 20:37–38, NIV

"The man without the Spirit does not accept the things that come from the Spirit of God, for they are foolishness to him, and he cannot understand them because they are spiritually discerned." —1 Corinthians 2:14, NIV

When it comes to salvation, there are different ways people come to God. Many who preach the Christian gospel have developed well-thought-out prayers and phrases to use when praying with someone seeking forgiveness for their sins. These formal prayers can be beautiful expressions of repentance and faith.

However, there are often times when no evangelist is present—moments when a person feels an urgent need to turn to God. In such cases, informal, personal prayers are just as powerful and pleasing to the Lord. What truly matters is the sincerity of the heart and the acknowledgment that Jesus is Lord and Savior, and belief in His death, burial, and resurrection.

There is a third kind of prayer: one that is unexpected, urgent, and unpolished—raw and immediate. This is the kind of prayer that has no time for eloquence. Consider the following example:

An avid atheist is flying his private plane home after an important business meeting. He smiles smugly, reflecting on how he manipulated the six men at the table—ruthless, cunning, and merciless. He had no remorse as he outmaneuvered his business partners, gaining the upper hand and increasing his wealth beyond imagination. He even laughed aloud as he recalled his closing remark: "It's my way or the highway." They had no choice but to give in.

But then, the smile vanishes. A sharp pain hits his chest—just left of center. He realizes with horror that he's having a heart attack. Control slips from his hands, and the plane begins to spiral downward. A grim smirk crosses his face. All that money—and now no time to enjoy it. And still, he scoffs at the idea of "God lovers."

Yet in these final moments, fear grips him. *What if hell is real? What if God exists?* As the ground rushes toward him, belief takes root. Seconds before the crash, the atheist cries out: "God, please forgive me!"

Two things happen at once.

First, his physical body is destroyed in the crash. Then, in a nanosecond, his spirit is in heaven—because the few seconds it took to ask for forgiveness were all the time needed for his sins to be transferred to the Lord Jesus Christ.

Many people wonder about the term *preordained.* God does not predestinate anyone for heaven or hell. However, because He exists outside of time, He sees each person's life in full view. He knows who will use their free will to seek Him and who will reject Him. God is never caught off guard or surprised.

"For a man's ways are in full view of the Lord, and He examines all his paths." —Proverbs 5:21, NIV

The only way to enter heaven is through God's Son, Jesus Christ.

And importantly, God does not discriminate. He shows no favoritism. All people—regardless of race, nationality, or status—are equal in His sight.

"Then Peter began to speak: 'I now realize how true it is that God does not show favoritism but accepts men from every nation who fear Him and do what is right.'" —Acts 10:34–35, NIV

To fear God and do what is right is to accept His Son, Jesus Christ, as Lord and Savior.

In the beginning, when God created the heavens and the earth, He called all of His creation *good*—except for one detail. What was it that God declared *not good*?

"The Lord God said, 'It is not good for the man to be alone. I will make a helper suitable for him." —Genesis 2:18, NIV

In the King James Version, this "suitable helper" is referred to as a *help meet*—someone who would help meet the needs of the man, Adam. In this situation, God did not choose to create another man, nor did He select some other type of creature to fulfill the role of helpmate. Instead, God chose to create a woman.

Though man and woman are physically different in many ways, God designed them for perfect companionship. Each was uniquely created for the other. They were meant to share a strong, natural, and eternal affinity. This union is the only type of intimate, physical relationship that the Lord God has approved.

A person, place, thing, or idea—these are known as nouns, and these are concepts established by God. But *transgender* is an idea of man that stands in direct opposition to God's will. It is a distortion of God's design—not inspired by the Spirit, but by demonic influence—and ultimately, it leads to destruction and separation from God.

"Jesus replied, 'I saw Satan fall like lightning from heaven.'" —Luke 10:18, NIV

Some believe that when Jesus made this statement, He was foretelling His future victory over Satan at the cross. However, Jesus was actually referring to a moment of divine authority— where Satan was cast out of heaven at His command.

"The great dragon was hurled down—that ancient serpent called the devil, or Satan, who leads the whole world astray. He was hurled to the earth, and his angels with him." —Revelation 12:9, NIV

There are people who believe they have committed such terrible sins that forgiveness is impossible. Because they cannot forgive themselves, they assume that God surely cannot either. As a result, they remain stuck in guilt and spiritual separation, never receiving the gift of being born again.

But let this truth be known: self-forgiveness is not a requirement for salvation. Only God's forgiveness can bring eternal life.

The Apostle Paul understood this. Before becoming a follower of Christ, Paul was responsible for the persecution—and even the deaths—of many early Christians. While the Bible doesn't explicitly say it, it's likely that Paul participated in the violent stonings of believers. And yet, Paul became a powerful witness of God's grace, mercy, and redemptive love.

No matter your past, God's forgiveness is greater than your guilt. Salvation is not dependent on how you feel about your past—it is dependent on whether you have accepted Jesus Christ as your Savior, repented of your sins, and believed in His resurrection.

"Everyone who calls on the name of the Lord will be saved." —Romans 10:13, NIV

"But one thing I do: forgetting what is behind and straining toward what is ahead, I press on toward the goal to win the prize for which God has called me heavenward in Christ Jesus." Philippians chapter 3, verses 13 through 14 NIV

Paul made the statement, "forgetting what is behind." It would have been impossible for him to forget such matters. However, Paul was comforted in knowing he had God's forgiveness, had been made new, and had a very important role to play in proclaiming the Good News of the Gospel. Paul understood that while he could not forget what was behind, he must not allow himself to focus on what was behind. The same opportunity is given to all who believe.

"Come to Me, all you who are weary and burdened, and I will give you rest. Take My yoke upon you and learn from Me, for I am gentle and humble in heart, and you will find rest for your souls. For My yoke is easy and My burden is light." Matthew chapter 11, verses 28 through 30 NIV

Through the Holy Spirit, Jesus is calling for the unsaved to come to Him and be joined together with Him. The heaviness of sin, fear of the unknown, and weariness in the search for unfound meaning will then be shared with Him. A restful feeling will flow from within, bringing peace and tranquility as you continue your journey—now not alone, but with the One who will lead you along the narrow path that leads to heaven.

There are many unthinkable sins, as previously discussed. Necrophilia, which is a sexual attraction to a human corpse and openly condoned by Islam, would be near the top of the list. However, another equally disgusting and horrifying sin is pedophilia. This is sexual attraction to young children and babies. These sickening urges are not fulfilled through self-induced physical functions to their own bodies, but by actual physical molestation. Young children, infants, and babies are subject to both physical and mental pain from which they might never recover while in the physical realm. Sadly, this is a state of our fallen world. Only God can bring goodness to the wickedness that abounds.

A gift is something that is given voluntarily without payment in return. "For it is by grace you have been saved, through faith—and this not from yourselves, it is the gift of God—not by works, so that no one can boast. For we are God's workmanship, created in Christ Jesus to do good works, which God prepared in advance for us to do." Ephesians chapter 2, verses 8 through 10 NIV

"For What It's Worth"

Song by Buffalo Springfield – Selected lyrics:

> There's something happening here, but what it is ain't exactly clear.
>
> There's a man with a gun over there, telling me I've got to beware.
>
> I think it's time we stop children, what's that sound?
>
> Everybody look, what's going down?

Our government has blatantly betrayed the people of America. During the mid-1970s, North and South Vietnam—which had been divided since 1954—were reunified. At that time, there were definitely men with guns over there telling us we should beware.

However, now the government of our republic, for a variety of reasons, has allowed men with guns and other weapons over here. These intruders hate America and want to see her downfall. When they think the time is right to do the most damage—both physical and political—they will strike. This will be similar to the attack on Israel on October 7, 2023. It will be demonically inspired, with unheard-of atrocities being committed.

America's only hope is God. We must ask His forgiveness for our turning from Him and excluding Him from our lives. Those from both political parties who have allowed the foolishness to happen must be removed. Election integrity is of the utmost importance. We must reinstate leaders who have proven they will follow through on warnings they give to America's enemies. That, along with extreme diligence to locate the intruders within America's borders, hopefully will lessen the threat of attack—though I fear we must experience some.

After the dust has settled from the election, we must never become complacent in regard to the threats we face. This was a problem Israel allowed to happen, and it contributed to a lack of readiness and rapid response to the surprise attack. This contributed to the high number of lives lost and hostages taken.

The following is a heartrending song that brings out two very important truths. Firstly, never miss the chance to tell someone you love them—the last time might be the last time you have the opportunity this side of heaven. Secondly, the lyrics to this song bring out the great love of Christ. His sacrifice on the cross assures all born-again believers that they will never be separated from each other in heaven.

"Scars in Heaven"

by Casting Crowns

(Songwriters: John Mark Hall, Matthew Joseph West / Source: LyricFind / Essential Music Publishing)

If I had only known the last time would be the last time

I would've put off all the things I had to do

I would've stayed a little longer, held on a little tighter

Now what I'd give for one more day with you

'Cause there's a wound here in my heart where something's missing

And they tell me that it's gonna heal with time

But I know you're in a place where all your wounds have been erased

And knowing yours are healed is healing mine

The only scars in heaven, they won't belong to me and you

There'll be no such thing as broken and all the old will be made new

And the thought that makes me smile now even as the tears fall down

Is that the only scars in heaven are on the hands that hold you now

I know the road you walked was anything but easy

You picked up your share of scars along the way

Oh, but now you're standing in the sun, you've fought your fight and your race is run

The pain is all a million miles away

The only scars in heaven, they won't belong to me and you

There'll be no such thing as broken and all the old will be made new

And the thought that makes me smile now even as the tears fall down

Is that the only scars in heaven, yeah, are on the hands that hold you now

Hallelujah, hallelujah

Hallelujah, for the hands that hold you now

There's not a day goes by that I don't see you

You live on in all the better parts of me

Until I'm standing with you in the sun, I'll fight this fight and this race I'll run

Until I finally see what you can see, oh-oh

The only scars in heaven, they won't belong to me and you

There'll be no such thing as broken and all the old will be made new

And the thought that makes me smile now even as the tears fall down

Is that the only scars in heaven are on the hands that hold you now.

How does one gain possession of the very precious key that leads to the wonders of Heaven? And after salvation has been attained and is yours forever, where does one keep this very precious key? Salvation is accomplished by asking God for the gift He has provided through His Son, Jesus Christ, and the key is kept in the heart.

"That if you confess with your mouth, Jesus is Lord, and believe in your heart that God raised Him from the dead, you will be saved. For it is with your heart that you believe and are justified; and it is with your mouth that you confess and are saved." Romans 10:9–10, NIV

In your own words, do this in a sincere and honest way, and you will have the following:

As the Scripture says, "Anyone who trusts in the Lord will never be put to shame." Romans 10:11, NIV

Once received, salvation can never be lost. Moments before His death, Jesus cried out, "It is finished," and it was finished. The precious blood that was shed for the true born-again believers was more than sufficient.

Before I was saved, I was a sinner. After I was saved, I'm a sinner. If salvation can be lost since I am a sinner, I would lose it many times while in the physical realm, either through thought or deed. Therefore, each time I sinned, I would have to again ask God for mercy through His Son.

This would greatly diminish Jesus' work on the cross, and He would have to go back to the cross for each sin I committed after my initial salvation experience. Add to that the fact that if salvation can be lost, we don't know if we, our family, or our friends are still saved—for it is possible to sin unknowingly and therefore not even realize we have fallen from grace.

For I am convinced that neither death nor life, neither angels nor demons, neither the present nor the future, nor any powers, neither height nor depth, nor anything else in all creation will be able to separate us from the love of God that is in Christ Jesus our Lord. Romans 8:38–39, NIV

A close encounter with the Holy Spirit will last through many valleys. While the initial mountaintop experience will wane, He will draw close again when you most need Him.

For those who believe, my prayer is that the promise of the wonders of Heaven will give you strength as you travel through this very sinful, fallen world.

For those not born again, I pray that the Holy Spirit will draw you to Jesus, you will repent and ask for forgiveness, and you will know and enjoy the wonders of Heaven.

God bless,

Burl L. Shepard

OTHER BOOKS
BY BURL L. SHEPARD

The Depth of the Riches: A Spiritual Adventure Based on Biblical Truths

The man found himself in a great valley, not remembering how he had arrived. As he began searching for answers, and after experiencing several strange events, he became convinced he had stumbled into an area of secret experimentation conducted by the government. Join him on his journey into the valley, where he discovers his destiny. A unique story of faith, hope, love, and truth.

A Son Is Given, A Child Is Born

A Son is given who, by His sacrificial blood, offers deliverance from sin. He will return—not as the sacrificial Lamb of God— but as the Ruler of all nations, ruling with an iron scepter as He provides never-ending peace and justice.

For It Is by Grace

Burl's third book is filled with thought-provoking truths regarding God's Word and the eternal fate of humanity.

Treasure of Truth: God Triumphant

Explore Christian apologetics and its significance to the Christian faith. Discover the power of God's Word and the only pathway to Heaven. What is the unforgivable sin—and what must one do to avoid committing it? Read about Israel, God's chosen people, and the growing apostasy of replacement theology. Learn God's purpose for the Ten Commandments. Go on a symbolic journey to Heaven and discover the wonders that may be waiting. Explore the new Heavens and the new Earth that God will create after the 1,000-year rule of Jesus on Earth. This book is uniquely written and deeply thought-provoking.

The Lord Is God

This book presents a unique blend of secular history and Christianity that leads to biblical truth. Topics include:

- Where does evil originate?
- Are demons real?
- The significance of World War I, World War II, the Munich Summer Olympics, the cruise ship *Achille Lauro*, and the 9/11 attack on America
- Psalm 91
- The Trinity
- David and Bathsheba
- Solomon's Temple and the Queen of Sheba
- Is there other intelligent life in the universe?
- What are UFOs?

- The Virgin Mary and Mary's song
- What is Heaven? What is Hell?
- The strongman Atlas
  ...and much more.

ABOUT THE AUTHOR

 Burl L. Shepard enjoyed a distinguished career marked by excellence, beginning with his work at National Life and Accident Insurance, where he earned prestigious awards and exclusive sales trips. His passion for service led him to spend 18 years in home healthcare with Apria Healthcare, where he made a lasting impact on countless families. He capped his stellar sales career at Mediacom Cable, consistently demonstrating dedication and integrity. Since retiring, Burl has devoted himself to an in-depth study of the Word of God, driven by a desire to deepen his faith and share insights that inspire others.